The Age of the Dinosaurs

Written by Jenny Vaughan
Illustrated by Simone Roberton

Collins Educational
An imprint of HarperCollinsPublishers

INTRODUCTION

Dinosaurs died out 65 million years ago but fossils offer proof that they existed. By studying fossils, scientists can attempt to deduce what dinosaurs were like. Most agree that dinosaurs belonged to the group of animals known as reptiles.

Fossilized teeth show that some dinosaurs ate plants, some ate meat and some probably ate both.

Fossilized bones show that some dinosaurs were small, fast-moving creatures, while others were the largest land animals that have ever lived. By studying the bones, scientists can determine what shape the dinosaurs were, how they moved and what they probably weighed.

Fossils provide a great deal of information, but there are still many many things not known about dinosaurs.

How a dead dinosaur becomes a fossil
1. The body lies on the ground or on a river bed. The flesh rots away leaving only the bones.
2. Layers of mud cover the skeleton, and exert pressure on it.
3. Over millions of years, the mud and the bones turn to rock and a fossilized dinosaur skeleton is formed.

Fossils
Fossils are the remains of plants, shells or bones from millions of years ago, often embedded in rock. Dinosaur fossils have been found from bones, scales from skin, footprints, eggs and droppings.

5000

4500
earth forms

Before the dinosaurs – the beginning of the earth
The earth began as a ball of gas with a core of hot, molten rock, about 4500 million years ago. There were no dinosaurs on earth when it first formed, in fact, there was no life at all.

During the first 1,000 million years, the earth cooled and became wetter, making it possible for living things to form. These first living things were so small that they would only have been visible through a microscope. Each was made up of just one living cell, and these single cell creatures lived in water.

Over the next few million years, living things became more complicated, larger and multi-cellular, evolving into the earliest plants and animals.

The amphibians arrive
By about 500 million years ago, fish and other sea creatures had developed from the first life forms. And about 400 million years ago, the first land plants evolved, followed by insects, spiders and amphibians.

Scientists believe that the first amphibians evolved from fish. Like the frogs and toads of today, these amphibians laid their eggs in water, but could exist on land.

Amphibians
Amphibians are animals which live in both in water and on land. Frogs, newts and toads are all amphibians. They lay their eggs in water, the eggs hatch out as tadpoles and gradually grow into adult animals which can then leave the water. Some of these early amphibians were much larger than those that exist today. Eryops, for example, was more than 2 metres long. Eryops lived in North America. It had small, sprawling legs and a flat head. It looked quite different from the small amphibians of today, such as frogs and newts, but fossils of early frogs show they may have descended from Eryops.

4000   3500

The reptiles arrive
About 280 million years ago, a new kind of animal evolved, the reptile. Reptiles descended from amphibians but they lived on land and did not lay their eggs in water.

Some of the first reptiles were the ancestors of lizards and turtles, some were the ancestors of the crocodiles and dinosaurs and some were the ancestors of mammals.

All reptiles have certain characteristics in common. They have dry, scaly skin, most of them lay eggs and they are cold-blooded. Being cold-blooded means their bodies cannot generate their own heat, so they need an outside source of heat (usually the sun) to give them energy.

Today, there are four different kinds of reptiles: turtles; crocodiles; lizards and snakes (so closely related they are classed as one kind); and the tuatara. The tuatara is a large, iguana-like reptile found only in New Zealand and which has a dorsal row of spines (a row of spines along its back).

Mammals evolve
Mammals evolved from reptiles into very different creatures. They are generally covered with fur or hair, the mothers produce milk in their bodies to feed their young and they are warm-blooded. Humans, elephants and whales are all mammals, although the first mammals were very small.

3500
earth begins to cool and first cells form

3000

The Age of the Dinosaurs

Dinosaurs evolved around 230 million years ago and remained on earth for nearly 200 million years.

Dinosaurs came in many shapes and sizes, and probably many colours, too. They lived on dry land all over the earth – in hot, dry places, on grassy plains and in forests and woodlands. None lived in water, though there were reptiles, such as plesiosaurs, which did. None could fly, either, though there were flying reptiles called pterosaurs. All these, like dinosaurs, are now extinct.

Not all the dinosaurs scientists have discovered lived at the same time. Some became extinct early on in the Age of the Dinosaurs. Some developed later, and some still existed 65 million years ago.

Scientists have gleaned this information from the rocks where they find the dinosaur fossils. It is possible to work out how old rocks are, and scientists know that any fossil bones embedded in the rocks must be the same age as the rock.

> The Ichthyosaur was a reptile that lived in the sea and ate fish. It was about 6 metres long and looked a bit like a dolphin. Ichthyosaurs were not the only sea-reptiles; others included plesiosaurs, which lived right until the end of the Age of the Dinosaurs. Pterosaurs were flying reptiles. There were many different kinds – some had a wing span as wide as a house, while others were much smaller.

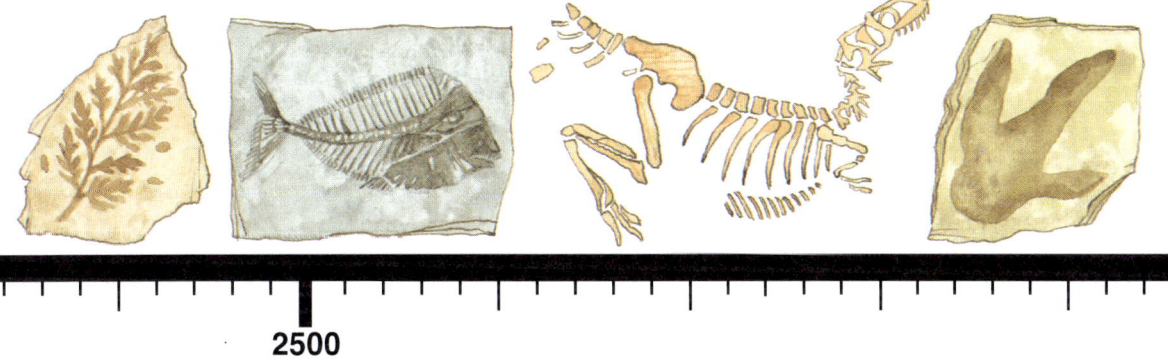

2500   2000

The world of the dinosaurs
At the beginning of the Age of the Dinosaurs, much of the land on earth was joined together in one huge continent, allowing dinosaurs to roam freely across the whole area. Gradually, sections of land broke away and oceans formed between them, resulting in fossils of the same kind of dinosaur being found on different continents.

During this time, the climate was warmer than today and stayed the same throughout the year, instead of changing with the seasons. There were rivers and seas, swamps and lakes, volcanoes and ranges of mountains which no longer exist.

There were few plants of the kind we know today. Most were giant ferns, fern-like plants called cycads, horsetails and conifers.

Conifers
Conifers are trees with needle-like leaves, which produce their seeds in cones. Fir trees are conifers. They have existed much longer than 'broad leafed' flowering trees such as oaks or sycamores.

DINOSAUR DATABANK

Only a few of the hundreds of different kinds of dinosaurs which existed are included on the following pages. Much of the information has been pieced together from studying clues, such as fossils and is, therefore, open to interpretation.

Shape and size

The biggest dinosaurs were two or three times as long as a bus, and much taller than a double-decker. The teeth of the biggest dinosaurs show that they were plant-eaters. It is likely their long necks enabled them to reach up to the topmost leaves of trees, as giraffes do today. Smaller dinosaurs could not reach these leaves and would eat from lower branches or the ground. Three of the largest and best-known giants were Apatosaurus (page 10), Brachiosaurus (page 13) and Diplodocus (page 16). These big plant-eaters often had beaks as well as teeth, probably for snipping off tough plant stems. The dinosaurs could then slice up the plants with their teeth.

Even larger were the dinosaurs named Supersaurus and Ultrasaurus, although few fossils have been found, little is known about them. They lived about 150 million years ago and both were 30 metres long. It is possible they weighed more than 70 tonnes – Ultrasaurus might have weighed as much as 130 tonnes.

More recently, scientists have found remains they believe came from two dinosaurs which they call Seismosaurus and Argentinosaurus, which were bigger still. But, again, there are very few fossils and experts cannot, yet, say much about them.

In contrast to these giant dinosaurs, there were many others that were often quite small and could move swiftly (see Coelophysis, page 14, Compsognathus, page 15 and Dromiceiomimus, page 17).

Colour
It is not known what colour dinosaurs were but reptiles today are often brightly-coloured, so some dinosaurs in this book have been shown as brightly-coloured, too.

Lizard hips or bird hips
Scientists divide dinosaurs into two catagories, the difference being their hip bones. Some had hip bones like the lizards of today, others had hip bones more like those of birds.

bird hip   lizard hip

Legs
The main difference between dinosaurs and other kinds of reptiles was their legs. A lizard's legs stick out sideways, so that when it runs along its stomach nearly touches the ground. Dinosaur's legs were more like the legs of a horse – they held the dinosaur's body up above the ground. No other kind of reptile had legs like these, and none do today.

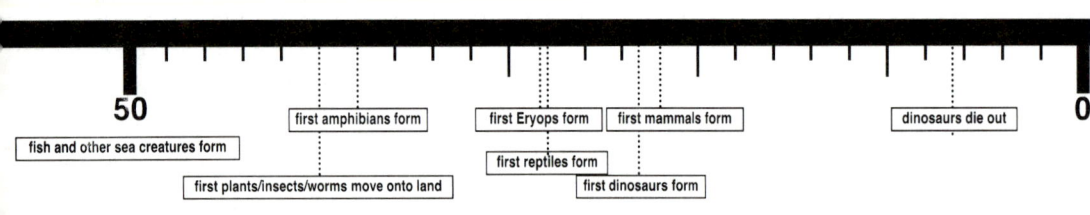

Living in herds

Many plant-eating dinosaurs lived in herds. Evidence for this is provided by the huge numbers of fossils found together. It is as if hundreds of dinosaurs all died at once – perhaps caught in a flood, or a landslide.

Hunters and fishers

Some dinosaurs had huge, jagged teeth and strong claws. These were the hunters, fishers and meat-eaters. Baryonyx (see page 12) is an example of a fish-eating dinosaur. Tyrannosaurus (page 24) lived at the very end of the Age of the Dinosaurs and is the best known meat-eater, but there were others, all living at different times, throughout the Age of the Dinosaurs.

In 1995, a new kind of dinosaur fossil was found in Argentina in South America. Only a few bones were found, but scientists think it was probably slightly bigger than Tyrannosaurus, which makes it the biggest meat-eating dinosaur fossil found so far. Because of this size, scientists named it Gigantosaurus. Gigantosaurus lived earlier than Tyrannosaurus – between 90 and 100 million years ago.

This timeline is an enlargement of pages 2-8.

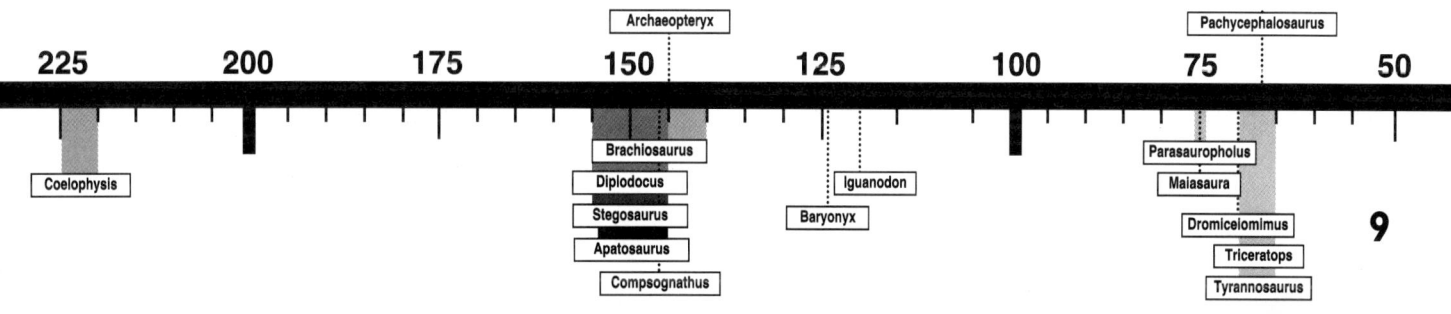

An A-Z of Dinosaurs

Name: .... **APATOSAURUS:** (a-<u>pat</u>-oe-<u>sor</u>-us) also known as Brontosaurus

Where fossils have been found: . North America

When it lived: . . . About 154–145 million years ago

Size: . . . . Length – about 21 metres
Weight – about 20 tonnes

Type: . . . . Lizard-hipped

Food type: . . . . . . Plant-eater

Many books refer to Apatosaurus as 'Brontosaurus'. Two names are used because, for a long time, scientists thought that two different Apatosaurus fossils which had been found were two different kinds of dinosaur. Apatosaurus was a plant-eater and among the largest land animals that has ever lived.

 x 2

Name:	**ARCHAEOPTERYX:** (<u>ar</u>-kee-<u>op</u>-ter-iks)
Where fossils have been found:	Northern Europe (Germany)
When it lived:	About 140 million years ago
Size:	Length – about 1 metre Weight – lighter than most dinosaurs its size
Type:	Lizard-hipped
Food type:	Fish-eater

Archaeopteryx looks like a small dinosaur from its fossil skeleton. But a close look at the fossil shows the outline of feathers surrounding the bones. Since Archaeopteryx was feathered, it was probably warm-blooded too – and its skeleton shows it could fly. In fact, although it looks very much like a dinosaur, and it is classed as 'lizard-hipped', it was the first known bird.

Archaeopteryx lived on tropical islands, and probably ate fish and other food picked up on the seashore.

x 1/10

Name:	**BARYONYX:** (<u>bar</u>-ee-<u>on</u>-iks)
Where fossils have been found:	England, possibly Africa
When it lived:	About 124 million years ago
Size:	Length – about 10 metres Weight – about 2 tonnes
Type:	Lizard-hipped
Food type:	Fish-eater

Baryonyx was a fish-eater. This is known because fossil fish-scales have been found in a Baryonyx fossil, where its stomach would have been. Its hooked claws may have been useful for scooping fish out of the water, and its teeth would be able to grip slippery scales.

 × 1

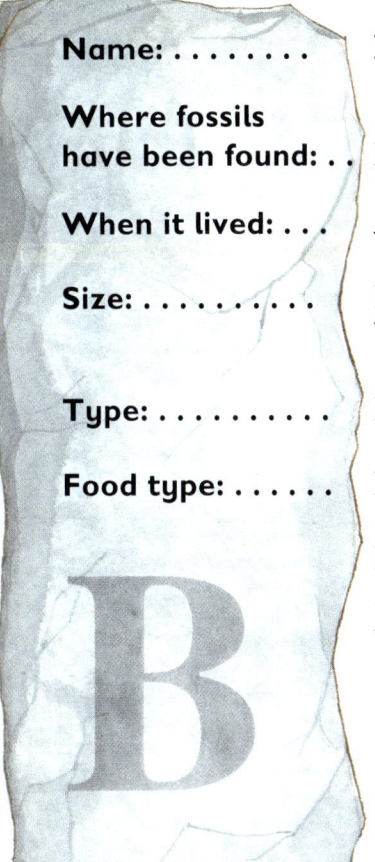

Name:	**BRACHIOSAURUS:** (brack-ee-oe-sor-rus)
Where fossils have been found:	East Africa and north America
When it lived:	About 155–140 million years ago
Size:	Length – about 23 metres Weight – about 50 tonnes
Type:	Lizard-hipped
Food type:	Plant-eater

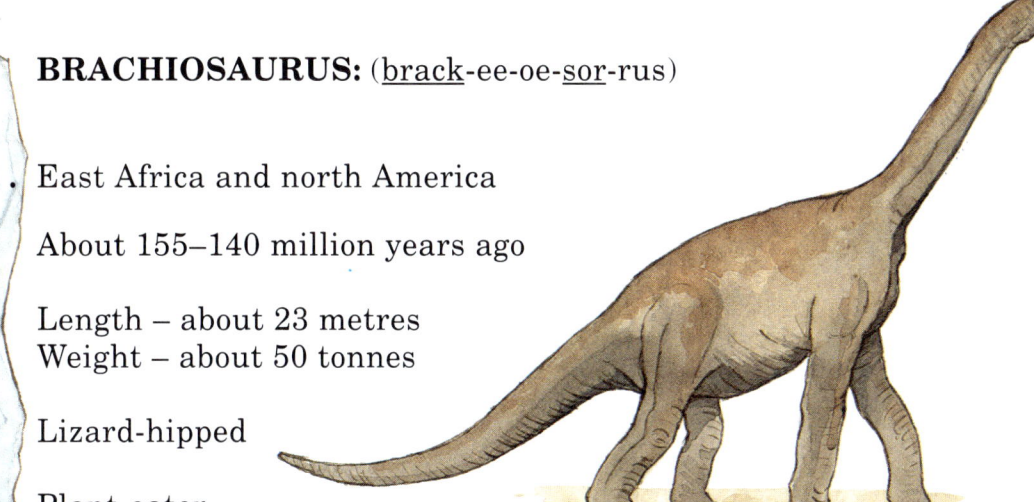

Brachiosaurus was one of the giant plant-eaters. Its long neck allowed it to browse on tree-tops. Fossils show that its teeth were worn down which might indicate a diet of tough leaves.

 x 3

Name:	**COELOPHYSIS:** (see-lo-fy-sis)
Where fossils have been found:	North America, Europe, east Asia
When it lived:	About 225–220 million years ago
Size:	Length – about 3 metres Weight – about 70 kilograms
Type:	Lizard-hipped
Food type:	Meat-eater

Coelophysis was one of the earliest dinosaurs. It was a hunter which could run swiftly to catch its prey. Fossil remains of small animals have been found in its stomach. It may even have been a cannibal – some fossils look as if they have the remains of smaller Coelophysis in their stomachs.

× 1/3

Name:	**COMPSOGNATHUS:** (<u>komp</u>-sog-<u>nath</u>-us)
Where fossils have been found:	Northern Europe
When it lived:	About 147 million years ago
Size:	Length – about 65 centimetres Weight – about 3 kilograms
Type:	Lizard-hipped
Food type:	Meat-eater

Compsognathus was capable of running fast. The sharp claws on its front feet were used to grab prey, which included other small reptiles and insects.

 × 1

Name:	**DIPLODOCUS:** (dip-<u>lod</u>-oe-kus)
Where fossils have been found:	North America, Europe, Africa, Asia
When it lived:	About 155–145 million years ago
Size:	Length – about 27 metres Weight – about 11 tonnes
Type:	Lizard-hipped
Food type:	Plant-eater

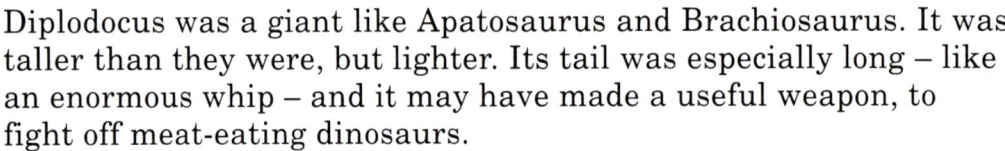

Diplodocus was a giant like Apatosaurus and Brachiosaurus. It was taller than they were, but lighter. Its tail was especially long – like an enormous whip – and it may have made a useful weapon, to fight off meat-eating dinosaurs.

 x 3

Name:	**DROMICEIOMIMUS:** (drome-ee-see-oe-mim-us)
Where fossils have been found:	North America
When it lived:	About 70 million years ago
Size:	Length – about 3.5 metres Weight – about 100 kilograms
Type:	Lizard-hipped
Food type:	Meat and plant-eater

Dromiceiomimus could probably run at more than 60 kilometres an hour – faster than any other dinosaur. It may have been a hunter, catching small reptiles and insects, but it probably ate plants as well. It had big eyes, with good eyesight, a sharp beak, and no teeth.

× 1/3

Name:	**IGUANODON:** (ig-<u>wa</u>-no-don)
Where fossils have been found:	Africa, Asia, Europe
When it lived:	About 120 million years ago
Size:	Length – about 10 metres Weight – about 5 tonnes
Type:	Bird-hipped
Food type:	Plant-eater

The Iguanodon skeleton was one of the very first to be discovered, but no-one then was quite sure how the bones fitted together. The Iguanodon had a spike on each front foot, but at first it was thought that the spike belonged on the end of its nose! Because there are places where many Iguanodon skeletons have been found together, scientists are almost certain that they lived in herds.

 x 1

Name:	**MAIASAURA:** (<u>my</u>-a-<u>sor</u>-ra)
Where fossils have been found:	North America
When it lived:	About 75 million years ago
Size:	Length – about 8 metres Weight – about 2 tonnes
Type:	Bird-hipped
Food type:	Plant-eater

Maiasaura's name means 'good mother reptile'. It has this name because so many fossil Maiasaura nests have been found with young in them. There are signs that Maiasaura cared for their young after they hatched, which is unusual for reptiles. The nests are in large groups, indicating whole herds of Maiasaura nested together, as some birds do today. They belonged to a group of dinosaurs called hadrosaurs, which lived in herds.

× 1

Name:	**PACHYCEPHALOSAURUS:** (<u>pack</u>-ee-<u>seff</u>-al-oe-<u>sor</u>-rus)
Where fossils have been found:	North America
When it lived:	About 67 million years ago
Size:	Length – about 10 metres Weight – about 2 tonnes
Type:	Bird-hipped
Food type:	Plant-eater

Pachycephalosaurus had a huge head, but that did not mean it had a large brain, just that its skull was about 25 cm thick. The male Pachycephalosaurus probably butted heads in fights over mates, just as many male animals living in herds do today.

Pachycephalosaurus's thick skull protected the brain in these fights, a bit like a huge motor cycle helmet. These dinosaurs lived in herds.

 × 1

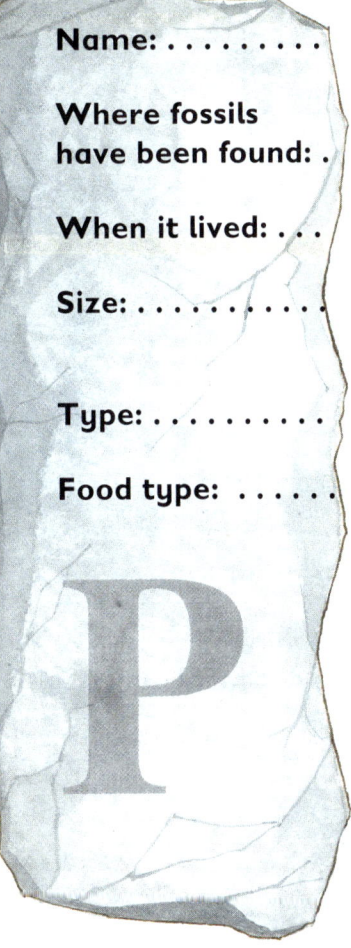

Name:	**PARASAUROPHOLUS:** (pa-ra-sorr-<u>off</u>-o-lus)
Where fossils have been found:	North America
When it lived:	About 76-74 million years ago
Size:	Length – about 10 metres Weight – about 2 tonnes
Type:	Bird-hipped
Food type:	Plant-eater

Parasauropholus lived in herds and had a tall crest on its head which would have helped them recognise their own kind. These crests may also have helped them to attract mates.

There were several different kinds of crested dinosaurs but Parasauropholus had the largest crest of all. Some scientists think it may have been able to blow air through its crest to make a hooting noise.

🚌 x 1

Name:	**STEGOSAURUS:** (steg-oe-sor-us)
Where fossils have been found:	North America, Africa
When it lived:	About 155–145 million years ago
Size:	Length – about 5 metres Weight – about 6 tonnes
Type:	Bird-hipped
Food type:	Plant-eater

The big plates on Stegosaurus's back may have been to protect it from enemies, or to help it get warm. Reptiles need warmth in order to move faster. If Stegosaurus stood sideways in the sunshine, the blood inside the plates could warm up quickly, and so provide heat for the dinosaur's whole body. Stegosaurus lived in herds.

 x 1/2

Name: .... **TRICERATOPS:** (try-ser-a-tops)

Where fossils have been found: . North America

When it lived: ... About 70–65 million years ago

Size: .... Length – about 9 metres
Weight – about 5.5 tonnes

Type: .... Bird-hipped

Food type: ..... Plant-eater

Triceratops's horns were probably for defence. It had a sharp beak for snipping off tough leaves. It probably lived in herds. Triceratops was one of the last of the dinosaurs and it died out with all the other dinosaurs on earth, 65 million years ago.

 x 1

Name: TYRANNOSAURUS: (tie-<u>ran</u>-oe-<u>sor</u>-us)

Where fossils have been found: North America

When it lived: About 70–65 million years ago

Size: Length – about 12 metres
Weight – about 6.5 tonnes

Type: Lizard-hipped

Food type: Meat-eater

Tyrannosaurus was a hunter. Its head was more than a metre long, and it was able to swallow a small dinosaur whole. It may have lain in wait for its prey and attacked suddenly because it would be unable to run very far or very fast.

 x 1

After the Dinosaurs

What happened?
The last remaining dinosaurs died out 65 million years ago. So did the sea-living plesiosaurs, and the flying pterosaurs.

Scientists are still not sure what happened to kill all the dinosaurs. The majority believe the climate of the world changed and it became too cold for dinosaurs to exist, or perhaps there was just not enough food for them.

One reason why the climate might have changed could have been that a huge meteorite hit the earth, filling the air with so much dust that the sun was blotted out. Violent volcanic explosions often change the weather today, so it follows that a huge meteorite would do a lot more damage than a volcano.

Whatever happened, it changed the world.

Mammals take over
Mammals had existed for about 150 million years when the dinosaurs died out. Until that time, they had been small, probably shy creatures which only came out at night when it was safe to look for insects and berries to eat.

Once the dinosaurs were extinct, new species of mammals began to evolve. Some of the early mammals died out completely, but others were the ancestors of creatures seen today.

Meteorites are lumps of rock from space. Most meteorites are quite small and burn up before they reach the ground, but every now and than, a big one reaches the earth. If one ended the Age of the Dinosaurs, it would have been enormous.

Dinosaur descendants live on

Mammals were not the only creatures to live on after the dinosaurs. There were smaller reptiles and amphibians, fish and millions of different kinds of insects. There were also some descendants of the dinosaurs themselves – the birds.

Birds might not seem very much like dinosaurs. They are, after all, usually small and light. But there are fossils that show that the very first bird, Archaeopteryx (see page 11), was so like a dinosaur, it was almost impossible to tell the difference. The only big difference between a fossil Archaeopteryx skeleton and any other dinosaur skeleton is that a pattern of feathers can be seen around the bones. Archaeopteryx had teeth in its mouth, claws on its front limbs and it may have been too heavy to fly far.

Other birds came after Archaeopteryx, but although they shared the sky with pterosaurs, such as Pteranodon, they were unrelated to them. The flying reptiles and all the dinosaurs died, but the birds survived. The Ichthyornis was one such bird which was 0.2 metres long, had webbed feet, a long beak and teeth. It looked a bit like a gull.

Dinosaur survivors?
All over the world stories are told of strange monsters which people think may be dinosaurs or some other ancient reptile. There have been reported sightings of a monster in Central Africa, another in a lake in Canada and another in a lake in Sweden. The most famous monster in the United Kingdom is the one that is supposed to live in Loch Ness.

There is no proof, however, that any of these creatures exist. Even if they did, none of the lake monsters could be dinosaurs, as dinosaurs lived on dry land.

No-one has ever caught one of these mystery reptiles, or taken a clear photograph of one. No-one has ever found their eggs, or the body of a dead one. There is no real evidence that dinosaurs or anything like them survived the unknown event that caused the end of the Age of the Dinosaurs, 65 million years ago.

Pronunciation guide:

Argentinosaurus: Arj-en-tin-oe-sor-rus
Eryops: er-ee-ops
Gigantosaurus: jie-gan-toe-sor-rus
Ichthyornis: ick-thee-or-nis
Ichthyosaur: ick-thee-oe-sor
Plesiosaur: pleez-ee-oe-sor
Pteranodon: ter-an-o-don
Pterosaur: ter-a-sor
Seismosaurus: size-moe-sor-rus
Supersaurus: soo-per-sor-rus
Ultrasaurus: ultra-sor-rus

Bibliography:

Benton, Dr Michael. *Dinosaurs and other Prehistoric Animals*, Kingfisher Factfinder, Kingfisher 1993

Czerkas, Sylvia J and Olson, Everett C, (editors). *Dinosaurs Past and Present, Volume I*, Natural History Museum of Los Angeles County in Association with University of Washington Press.

Czerkas, Sylvia J and Olson, Everett C, (editors). *Dinosaurs Past and Present, Volume II*, Natural History Museum of Los Angeles County in Association with University of Washington Press.

Eyewitness Dinosaur, Eyewitness Guides, Dorling Kindersley 1989

Gardom, Tim and Milner, Dr Angela. *The Natural History Museum Book of Dinosaurs*, Virgin Books 1993

Lambert, David, and the Diagram Group. *Dinosaur Data Book*, Facts on File in association with the British Museum (Natural History)

Pollock, Steve. *Dinosaurs*, BBC Factfinders, BBC Educational Publishing 1990

Russell, Dale A. *An Odyssey in Time: The Dinosaurs of North America*, The University of Toronto Press, in Association with the National Museum of Natural Sciences, Canada 1989

Index:

Africa 12, 16, 18, 22
    central 27
    east 13
America
    north 3, 10, 13, 14, 16, 17, 19, 20, 21, 22, 23
    south 9
amphibian 3, 4, 8, 26
Apatosaurus 7, 9, 10, 16
Archaeopteryx 9, 11, 26
Argentina 9
Argentinosaurus 7, 28
Asia 16, 18
    east 14
Baryonyx 9, 12
beak 7, 17, 23, 26
bird 8, 11, 19 26
bird-hip 8, 18, 19, 20, 21, 22, 23
bone 2, 5, 8, 9, 11, 18, 26
Brachiosaurus 7, 9, 13, 16
brain 20
Brontosaurus (see Apatosaurus)

Canada 27
cannibal 14
cell 3, 4
claw 9, 12, 15, 26
climate (see weather)
Coelophysis 8, 9, 14
cold-blooded 4
colour 5, 8
Compsognathus 8, 9, 15
conifer 6
crocodile 4
cycad 6
dinosaur 2, 3, 4, 5, 6, 7, 8, 9, 10, 11, 14, 16, 17, 19, 21, 22, 23, 24, 25, 26, 27
Diplodocus 7, 16
Dromiceiomimus 8, 9, 17
droppings 2
egg 3, 4, 27
enemy (ies) 22
England 12
Eryops 3, 8, 28
Europe 11, 14, 15, 16, 18
    north 15
eyesight 17

feathers 11, 26
fern 6
fish 3, 5, 8, 11, 12, 26
fish-eater 9, 11, 12
fisher 9
flood 9
food
    berry (ies) 25
    meat 2
    plant 2, 3, 6, 7, 17
footprint 2
fossil 2, 3, 5, 6, 7, 8, 9, 10, 11, 12, 13, 14, 15,
    16, 17, 18, 19, 20, 221, 22, 23, 24, 26
frog 3
Germany 11
giant 6, 7, 8, 13, 16
Gigantosaurus 9, 28
hadrosaurs 19
head 2, 3, 20, 24
herd 9, 18, 19, 20, 21, 22, 23
horn 23
horsetail 6
hunter 9, 14, 17, 24
Ichthyornis 26, 28

Ichthyosaur 5, 28
Iguanodon 9, 18
insect 3, 8, 15, 17, 25, 26
lake 6, 27
land 2, 3, 4, 5, 6, 7, 8, 10, 27
landslide 9
leg 3, 8
lizard 4, 8
lizard hip 8, 10, 11, 12, 13, 14, 15, 16,
    17, 24
Loch Ness 27
Maiasaura 9, 19
mammal 4, 5, 8, 25, 26
meat (see food)
meat-eater 9, 14, 15, 16, 17, 24
meteorite 25
multi-cellular 3
neck 7, 13
nest 19
newt 3
New Zealand 4
ocean 6
Pachycephalosaurus 9, 20
Parasauropholus 9, 21

31

plant-eater 7, 9, 10, 13, 16, 17, 18, 19, 20, 21,
            22, 23
Plesiosaurs 5, 25, 28
Pteranodon 26, 28
Pterosaur 5, 25, 28
reptile 2, 4, 5, 8, 15, 17, 19, 22, 26, 27
         flying 5, 26
         sea 5
rock 2, 3, 5, 25
scales
scientist 2, 5, 7, 8, 9, 10, 18, 21, 25
Seismosaurus 7, 28
skeleton 2, 11, 18, 26
skin 2, 4
snake 4
spider 3
Stegosaurus 9, 22
Supersaurus 7, 28
Sweden 27
tadpole 3
teeth 2, 7, 9, 12, 13, 17, 26
Triceratops 9, 23
Tuatara 4
Tyrannosaurus 9, 24

Ultrasaurus 7, 28
United Kingdom 27
warm-blooded 4, 11
weather 10, 25
wing span 5
whale 4